YOU'RE NOT BROKEN

YOU'RE JUST FIGHTING
THE WRONG BATTLE

DAERON MYERS

THE REAL WAR

You wake up every day with the best intentions.

You tell yourself, *"Today I'm going to be different."*
More focused.
More disciplined.
More patient.
More consistent.
More like the person you know you're capable of becoming.

But somehow… you keep ending up in the same place.

Same habits.
Same reactions.
Same cycles.
Same patterns that you swore you were done with.

And after a while, a quiet question starts to form inside:

"What's wrong with me?"

Most people think the battle is outside of them.
They blame circumstances.

They blame people.
They blame bad luck.
They blame the environment.
They blame the past.

But the truth is deeper.

The real war has never been around you.
It has always been within you.

There is an inner voice that sabotages.
An old program that reacts.
A wounded part that protects.
A survival system that no longer fits the
life you are trying to build.

It's not that you're broken.
It's not that you're weak.
It's that you've been fighting the wrong enemy.

You've been aiming your energy at the world,
when the real battlefield has been your mind, your
emotions, your beliefs, and your identity.

This book is not about motivation.
It's about **liberation**.

It will help you:

- Recognize the inner saboteur that has been running your life
- Understand the wounds that shaped your reactions
- Disarm the beliefs that keep you stuck
- Rebuild your identity from the inside out
- And finally win the war that matters most

Because once you stop fighting yourself,
once you heal what's been hurting,
once you silence what's been lying,
once you align who you are with who you're becoming…

Nothing can stand in your way.

This is not a book about changing your circumstances.
This is a book about changing your **inner command center**.

And when that changes…
Your entire life follows.

CONTENTS

Chapter 1

THE WAKE-UP CALL

When a child learns he is not disposable, even when the world makes him feel like he is.

Daeron was nine years old when his world cracked.

Up until then, his life had a center.
Her name was Aunt Gladys.

She wasn't just an aunt.
She was safety.
She was routine.
She was the one who showed up.
She was the one who raised him, fed him,
corrected him, hugged him, and made him feel
like he belonged somewhere in this world.

So when custody was handed over to a father who had just come home from ten years in prison, it didn't feel like a legal decision.

It felt like abandonment.

It felt like being handed off.

It felt like, *"You're no longer wanted here."*

Moving into his father's house with Kristy was not comfort.
It was unfamiliar.
It was unstable.
It was loud with arguments, betrayal, tears, and tension.
He watched his stepmother cry.
He felt the energy of infidelity, broken trust,
and emotional chaos in the air.

And inside a nine-year-old boy's heart, a dangerous belief began
to form:

"If the woman who raised me could let me go…
Then maybe nobody really wants me."

He didn't trust his father yet.
He didn't feel safe emotionally.
He didn't feel rooted.
He felt like a burden passed from one adult to another.

And the voice started:

"No one really cares about you."
"You're on your own."
"You better learn how to survive."
"You're just in the way."

Those thoughts didn't come as sentences.
They came as feelings.
Tight chest.
Heavy stomach.

Lonely walks.
Silence that felt louder than noise.

He would take solo walks, carrying emotions too big for a child's
body.
And eventually the pain grew so heavy that
reckless thoughts began to form.

"What if I wasn't here anymore?"
"Would anyone even notice?"

That is not rebellion.
That is a wounded child asking if his life has value.

And then something changed.

Not in a quiet room.
Not in therapy.
Not in a church pew.

But at a cookout.

Laughter in the air.
Plates in hands.
Music playing.

And Uncle Nard stood up and spoke words that rewired a destiny:

"Daeron is going to be somebody."

He didn't whisper it.
He didn't doubt it.
He declared it.

In front of people.
In front of witnesses.
In front of a boy who secretly believed he didn't matter.

That was the first time the old voice was challenged.

Then came Wise Men Salute.
Then Uncle Bird.
Then Uncle Ron.
Then mentorship.

And Uncle Nard said something that became a spiritual seed:

"I'm rubbing knowledge in your head. You can make something of yourself."

In that moment, a new belief began forming:

"Maybe I'm not broken.
Maybe I'm just undeveloped.
Maybe I'm growing.
Maybe I need guidance, not condemnation.
Maybe mentors are my GPS."

That was Daeron's wake-up call.

Not just to pain…
But to purpose.

How to Know This Is Your Chapter

This chapter is about you if:

- You experienced abandonment early
- You felt like a burden instead of a blessing
- You learned to survive instead of being nurtured
- You struggle with trust
- You walk alone when emotions get heavy
- You battle thoughts of "Do I even matter?"
- You crave guidance but never had consistent mentorship

What Was Really Happening

At nine years old, your nervous system learned:

"Love leaves."
"Stability can be taken."
"I have to fend for myself."

This creates:

- Hyper-independence
- Emotional walls
- Overachieving or self-sabotage
- A constant need to prove worth

You weren't broken.
You were developing without a map.

DAILY HEALING PRACTICE – REPARENTING THE NINE-YEAR-OLD

Morning Practice (5 minutes)

Place your hand on your chest and say:

"I am not a burden.
I am becoming.
I am guided.
I am protected."

Ask in writing:
"What does the 9-year-old version of me need today?"

When Abandonment Is Triggered

When you feel:

- Rejected
- Overlooked
- Disrespected
- Emotionally alone

Do this:

1.   Pause and breathe slowly.
2.   Say: "This is old pain, not present danger."
3.   Visualize someone saying: "You're going to be somebody."
4.   Repeat: "I am guided. I am growing. I am not alone."

Night Practice – Mentor Activation

Write one page answering:

- What did I learn today?
- Who spoke life into me today?
- What wisdom did I receive?

Even if it came from a book, a video, or God.

Mentorship doesn't only come in bodies.
It comes in voices, words, and alignment.

7-DAY RESET: FROM ABANDONED TO ANCHORED

This 7-day practice is for anyone who has ever felt unwanted, overlooked, or emotionally alone. Each day builds safety, identity, and inner strength.

Day 1 – Tell the Truth

Write your childhood story around the moment you first felt abandoned, rejected, or misunderstood.
Don't edit it. Don't minimize it. Just tell it honestly.

Ask yourself:

- When did I first feel "on my own" emotionally?
- What did I start believing about myself that day?

Day 2 – Name the Wound

Write down the core belief that formed from that moment, such as:

- "I'm not important."
- "People leave."
- "I have to survive by myself."
- "I'm a burden."

Seeing the belief weakens its control.

Day 3 – Release the Unspoken

Write a letter to the person or situation that hurt you.
Say everything you never got to say.
You are not writing to send — you are writing to free your heart.

Day 4 – Reparent Yourself

Write a letter to your younger self from your current self.

Tell them:

- You are safe now.
- You are not alone.
- You are loved.
- You are growing, not broken.

Day 5 – Install New Truth

Create 5 new identity statements to replace the old belief, such as:

- I am worthy of love.
- I am guided, not abandoned.
- I am becoming, not broken.
- I am protected.
- I am valuable.

Read them aloud morning and night.

Day 6 – Seek Guidance

Identify at least one source of mentorship or wisdom:

- A book
- A teacher
- A coach
- A spiritual leader
- A positive role model

Commit to learning from them daily, even if it's 10 minutes.

Day 7 – Declare Your Direction

Write a one-page vision of the person you are becoming.

Answer:

- Who am I growing into?
- What kind of man/woman will I be emotionally?
- How will I treat myself differently?
- What willI no longer tolerate?

Then read it aloud as a declaration.

LIFE LESSON

Abandonment did not define you.
It positioned you.

God didn't remove you.
He redirected you.

And mentors became your GPS because your destiny was too big
to navigate alone.

LIFE LESSON PRAYER

"God,
Heal the younger child in me who felt unwanted,
unprotected, and unsure of his place in this world.

Thank You for the people who loved me.
Thank You for __(fill in the blank with someone
special)_____, and the Wise humans who spoke life into me.
Thank You for mentors who became my spiritual coordinates.

Silence the lie that says I am a burden.
Strengthen the truth that says I am becoming.
Guide me like a GPS toward the life You designed for me.

I am not abandoned.
I am being built.
I am not forgotten.
I am being prepared.
I am not alone.
I am guided.

Amen."

Chapter 2

SURVIVAL TO SIGHT

When the hustler mindset gives way to a vision for a bigger life.

Daeron learned early that nobody was coming to save him.

After the move, after the chaos, after being shifted from house to house, something inside him hardened—not in a cruel way, but in a protective way. A nine-year-old boy had quietly made a decision: *I'm going to take care of myself.*

And that decision shaped everything.

By his teenage years, survival had become identity.

Not survival as in barely eating.
Survival as in *get it how you live.*
Survival as in *if you want something, you take it.*
Survival as in *don't depend on nobody but you.*

While other kids were worried about clothes and parties, Daeron was worried about stability, respect, and money. He learned the language of the streets. He learned how to move. He learned how to read people. He learned how to hustle.

Selling drugs.
Stealing.
Robbing.

Not because he was evil.
Because he was in survival mode.

And survival mode doesn't ask, *Is this right?*
It asks, *Will this work? Will this keep me
safe? Will this keep me ahead?*

But something in his spirit never fully went numb.

After one robbery, when the adrenaline wore off, guilt sat heavy
in his chest.
This isn't me, he thought.
He felt the weight of what he could become
if he stayed on that road.

Then came the moment that burned itself into his memory.

The jump-out boys.

Police jumping out of unmarked cars.
Chaos.
Someone tossing their pack on the ground.
Hands on the wall.
A ride to the station.
Hours in a holding cell.

Sitting there, the cold bench against his back, the walls too close,
the air thick with consequences, a terrifying realization hit him:

If I don't change, I'm going to end up exactly where my father and older brothers ended up. Prison. Cycles. Lost years.

That cell wasn't just a room.
It was a mirror.

And for the first time, Daeron didn't just see where he was.
He saw where he was headed.

Later, life shifted again.

New York.

New environment.
No familiar streets.
No old friends.
No comfort zone.

Just him, football, and teammates who talked about the *next level* instead of the next hustle. Coaches like CT Chatham who didn't just train bodies—they spoke to futures.

Then came exposure.

Skyscrapers.
Opportunity.
Different kinds of success.

Working at JPMorgan Chase, he met people who owned businesses, who invested, who built, who traveled, who thought globally. He saw Black excellence up close in the form of Papi Bill and Grandma Sheila—successful, peaceful, with a pool in the backyard and a life that looked nothing like struggle.

And a truth hit him hard:

My world has been a mustard seed. The world is a harvest.

There was more.
So much more.

And survival thinking was too small to contain destiny.

HOW TO KNOW THIS CHAPTER IS ABOUT YOU

This chapter speaks to you if:

- You grew up in "get it how you live" mode
- You trust yourself more than anyone
- You learned to hustle before you learned to dream
- You believe money equals safety
- You've done things you're not proud of just to survive
- You fear ending up like people in your past
- You feel there's more for your life but don't fully know how to reach it yet

WHAT'S REALLY HAPPENING

Survival mode teaches:

- "I can't depend on anyone."
- "The world is dangerous."
- "I have to stay ahead or I'll fall behind."
- "Fast money is better than no money."

But vision mode teaches:

- "I can build, not just get by."
- "I can choose long-term over short-term."
- "I can create a different story."
- "I am not limited to my environment."

Awareness is the bridge between the two.

DAILY PRACTICE – FROM HUSTLE TO VISION

Morning: Identity Reset (5 minutes)

Say aloud:

"I am not in survival.
I am in alignment.
I am building a future, not just getting through today."

Journal:

- What am I afraid of losing?
- What am I afraid of becoming?
- What am I truly meant to build?

When Old Survival Triggers Hit

When you feel:

- The urge to rush
- The urge to prove
- The urge to take shortcuts
- The urge to control everything

Do this:

1. Pause your body with slow breathing.
2. Ask: "Is this survival or vision talking?"
3. Choose the long-term move, not the fast one.
4. Repeat: "I am safe enough to build, not just hustle."

Evening: Exposure Upgrade

Every night, expose your mind to:

- A story of success
- A business video
- A leadership message
- A mentor's words

What you see expands what you believe is possible.

7-DAY SHIFT: FROM SURVIVAL TO BUILDER

Day 1: Write the survival rules you learned.

Day 2: Write the cost those rules have had on your peace.

Day 3: Write the life you actually want to live.

Day 4: Identify one habit that keeps you in "street mode."

Day 5: Replace it with one "builder habit."

Day 6: Study someone who has the life you want.

Day 7: Declare out loud: "I am no longer limited
by my past environment."

LIFE LESSON

You were never meant to stay in survival.

Survival kept you alive.
But vision is what will make you free.

Exposure is the doorway.
Awareness is the key.
Choice is the power.

LIFE LESSON PRAYER

"God,
Thank You for keeping me alive in seasons where I had to survive.
Thank You for protecting me when I didn't even know how to protect myself.

Now open my eyes to what is possible.
Break the limits of my old environment.
Shift my mind from hustle to vision,
from short-term to legacy,
from reaction to intention.

Place mentors, coaches, and examples in my life that stretch me.
Let me see the world the way You see it—full of opportunity, growth, and purpose.

I am no longer trapped in survival.
I am stepping into the life You prepared for me.

Amen."

Chapter 3

CHANGING THE STORY

The moment you realize you are not who your past says you are, but who your future is calling you to become.

For most of his early life, Daeron carried a quiet label inside.

Not one anyone pinned on his chest.
One that lived in his own thoughts.

I'm a knucklehead.
I'm a can't-get-right.
I'm the one who always messes up.

It wasn't spoken out loud often, but it was felt every day.

Where he came from, a stop at jail wasn't shocking.
It was almost expected.
It was part of the environment.
Part of the rhythm of life.

Men disappeared for months.
Sometimes years.
Sometimes forever.

So in his mind, the future looked narrow.
Limited.
Predictable.

Not because he wanted it that way…
But because that's all he had ever seen.

Then something happened that cracked the old story wide open.

He applied for a job at JPMorgan Chase.

No experience.
No corporate background.
No blueprint.

Just hunger.

He wrote his own resume.
Filled out application after application.
Showed up when most people from his
environment wouldn't even think to apply.

And then… he got the job.

A building.
A badge.
Dress clothes.
Professional language.

Structure.
Standards.

It felt like walking into another world.

And for the first time, he saw himself in a mirror that didn't
reflect survival —
It reflected *potential*.

Then came Steve Fernelis.

A New York slick-talker with vision in his voice.

One day Steve said something that shifted everything:

"We're not going to be selling stocks, bonds, and mutual funds
forever.
One day, we're going to *be* the wealth management clients."

That sentence did something inside Daeron.

It wasn't about money.
It was about identity.

Someone from a different world was looking at him and seeing
ownership, not labor.
Seeing *future*, not background.
Seeing *legacy*, not limitation.

And suddenly, the old lie began to crack:

I'm unqualified.
I'm cursed.
People like me don't make it.

He realized that belief had been passed down like a family heirloom of limitation.
A story told so many times it started sounding like truth.

But it wasn't truth.

It was permission to stay small.

And Daeron refused it.

A new belief rose up:

I am the chosen one.
I'm better than what I've been displaying.
Poverty ran in my family until it ran into me.

Changing the story didn't just mean making more money.

It meant:

Being a better father.
Being a better man.
Being a builder, not just a worker.
Owning, not just doing.
Breaking cycles, not repeating them.

It meant unlocking something in the family tree so the next generation could point and say:

"It's possible. He did it. So can we."

HOW TO KNOW THIS CHAPTER IS ABOUT YOU

This chapter is for you if:

- You grew up with labels that said "trouble," "failure," or "not enough"
- You expect setbacks because that's all you've ever seen
- You secretly believe success is for "other people"
- You feel called to break generational patterns
- You want to be the first, not the next statistic
- You know deep down you're meant for more than survival

WHAT'S REALLY HAPPENING

Every family carries a story.

Some stories say:

- "We always struggle."
- "We never get ahead."
- "We're not built for wealth."
- "Success isn't for people like us."

But one person can rewrite the narrative.

The chosen one is not the favorite.
The chosen one is the *cycle breaker*.

DAILY PRACTICE – REWRITING THE INNER SCRIPT

Morning: Identity Declaration

Say aloud:

"I am not my environment.
I am not my past.
I am not my family's limitations.
I am the one who changes the story."

Write:

- What story did I inherit?
- What story am I choosing to create?

Midday: Vision Rehearsal

For 3 minutes, close your eyes and picture yourself:

- Owning instead of just working
- Leading instead of following
- Teaching instead of surviving
- Building something that outlives you

Your brain must see it before your life can build it.

Evening: Legacy Reflection

Ask:

- What did I do today that aligned with the person I'm becoming?
- What would the future version of me be proud of today?

7-DAY BELIEF RESET

Day 1: Write every negative label you've ever accepted.

Day 2: Write the truth that replaces each one.

Day 3: Study one person who broke generational cycles.

Day 4: Speak your future out loud for 10 minutes.

Day 5: Eliminate one habit that keeps you small.

Day 6: Install one habit that builds your future.

Day 7: Declare: "The cycle stops with me."

LIFE LESSON

You are not here to continue the story.
You are here to *change* it.

Poverty, limitation, and fear may have run in your family…
But they ran into you.

And they met their end.

LIFE LESSON PRAYER

"God,

Thank You for choosing me to break what has bound my family for generations.

Remove every lie that says I am unqualified, cursed, or limited.

Plant the truth deep in my spirit:

I am chosen.

I am capable.

I am called to build, not just survive.

Let my life be proof that cycles can be broken,

that vision can replace fear,

and that legacy can rise from pain.

Use me as the one who changes the story.

Not just for myself…

But for everyone who comes after me.

Amen."

Chapter 4

THE POWER OF MENTORSHIP

When guidance enters your life and shows you the road you could never see by yourself.

For a long time, Daeron believed strength meant figuring everything out alone.

Life had taught him that.
When you're moved around as a child…
When adults are unstable…
When the environment is unpredictable…
You learn to rely on yourself.

You learn to say, *"I got it."*
Even when you don't.

But self-reliance, when it goes too far, turns into isolation.
And isolation makes the journey longer, harder,
and more painful than it has to be.

Daeron had vision, hunger, and drive.
But what he didn't have yet was *direction*.

He was moving…
But he wasn't always sure where.

Then mentors started showing up.

Not perfect men.
Not flawless people.
But men with perspective.

Uncle Nard.
Uncle Bird.
Uncle Ron.
Wise Men Salute.
Coach CT Chatham.
Steve at JPMorgan.
Papi Bill.
Grandma Sheila.

Each one carried a piece of the map.

They didn't just talk about money.
They talked about *mindset*.
They didn't just talk about success.
They talked about *character*.
They didn't just talk about where you are.
They talked about where you could go.

Uncle Nard's words echoed like a spiritual assignment:

"I'm rubbing knowledge in your head. You can make something of yourself."

That wasn't casual conversation.
That was identity being installed.

Mentorship didn't just give Daeron information.
It gave him **permission to see himself differently.**

When Coach CT pushed the team, it wasn't just about football.
It was about discipline.
Structure.
Standards.
The belief that you could reach a level you'd never seen before.

When Steve at JPMorgan spoke about becoming wealth management clients one day, it shifted something internal:

I don't just work in these buildings… I belong in rooms like this.

When Papi Bill and Grandma Sheila lived well, peacefully, successfully, it silently said:

This life is possible for us too.

Mentorship expanded his *imagination*.

And imagination is the womb of destiny.

HOW TO KNOW THIS CHAPTER IS ABOUT YOU

This chapter is for you if:

- You feel like you're figuring life out the hard way
- You are strong but tired of being alone in the process
- You crave guidance but don't know who to trust
- You know you're meant for more but lack a clear roadmap
- You've never really had consistent, wise leadership
- You want to grow but don't want to repeat the same mistakes

WHAT'S REALLY HAPPENING

Without mentorship, people rely on:

- Trial and error
- Pain as a teacher
- Time as their only guide

With mentorship, you receive:

- Shortcuts in wisdom
- Protection from unnecessary mistakes
- Perspective beyond your environment
- A vision for who you can become

Mentors are spiritual GPS systems.
They don't drive the car for you.
They show you the turns before you crash.

DAILY PRACTICE – ACTIVATING GUIDANCE

Morning – Humility Prayer (3 minutes)

Say:

"God, send the right voices into my life.
I am teachable.
I am open.
I am ready to grow."

Midday – Wisdom Intake

Every day, expose yourself to *one* source of wisdom:

- A book chapter
- A podcast
- A sermon
- A mentor's video
- A coaching call

Growth is not accidental.
It is scheduled.

Evening – Reflection

Write:

- What did I learn today?
- How can I apply it tomorrow?
- Who am I becoming by learning this?

7-DAY MENTOR ALIGNMENT PLAN

Day 1: Identify the areas you need guidance (money, mindset, relationships, discipline, faith, leadership).

Day 2: List people you admire in those areas.

Day 3: Follow, read, or study one of them intentionally.

Day 4: Reach out for guidance or mentorship (DM, email, program, book).

Day 5: Apply one piece of advice immediately.

Day 6: Reflect on what changed.

Day 7: Commit to a season of learning and submission to growth.

LIFE LESSON

Your future is too important to navigate without a map.

Mentors don't make you small.
They make you sharp.

They don't control your destiny.
They reveal it.

LIFE LESSON PRAYER

"God,
Thank You for the men and women You place in our lives to guide us.
Thank You for mentors who see what we cannot yet see,
and who speak life when our vision is limited.

Give me a teachable heart.
Remove pride that says I must figure everything out alone.
Align me with wisdom, with guidance, with destiny connections.

Let the right voices shape me,
correct me,
stretch me,
and prepare me for the life You have called me to build.

I am not walking alone.
I am guided.
I am growing.
I am becoming.

Amen."

Chapter 5

HEALING THE WOUND OF WORTH

When you finally learn that your value was never tied to what you survived, what you did, or what people failed to give you.

For a long time, Daeron moved like a man who knew how to get things done…
but deep inside, there was still a boy asking a quiet question:

"Am I enough?"

Not enough to hustle.
Not enough to survive.
Not enough to be strong.

Enough to be loved.
Enough to be chosen.
Enough to be secure without proving.

When a child experiences abandonment, chaos, or instability, the wound that forms is not just emotional—it becomes identity. The heart starts to believe:

"I must earn love."
"I must perform to matter."
"I must become something to be worthy."

So Daeron became driven.
Focused.
Relentless.

But beneath the ambition was a deeper hunger:
To finally feel solid inside. To finally feel like he belonged in the world, not just in the grind.

Success began to come.
Opportunities opened.
Respect grew.

Yet there were still moments when silence felt heavy.
When rest felt uncomfortable.
When slowing down felt unsafe.

Because when you grow up in survival, stillness can feel like danger.

And healing requires stillness.

It requires sitting with the younger version of yourself and telling him the truth no one told him:

"You were never a burden."
"You were never too much."

"You were never unwanted."
"You were just a child in a world that
didn't know how to protect you."

This is where worth is rebuilt—not in accomplishments, but in
compassion.

HOW TO KNOW THIS CHAPTER IS ABOUT YOU

This chapter is for you if:

- You feel like you always have to prove your value
- You tie your worth to productivity or success
- You feel uneasy when you rest
- You fear being seen as "not enough"
- You crave validation even when you're winning
- You struggle to receive love without questioning it

WHAT'S REALLY HAPPENING

Your nervous system learned:

"I am safe when I am useful."
"I am loved when I perform."
"I matter when I produce."

But your soul is learning:

"I am worthy because I exist."
"I am loved because I am."
"I am enough without effort."

Healing worth means separating identity from achievement.

DAILY PRACTICE – REBUILDING INNER WORTH

Morning: Worth Declaration

Look in the mirror and say:

"I am worthy of love, rest, peace, and success.
Not because of what I do.
But because of who I am."

Write one page answering:

- What am I trying to prove?
- Who am I trying to impress?
- What would it feel like to just *be* enough?

Midday: Nervous System Reset

When you feel the urge to overwork or overprove:

1. Pause.
2. Place your hand on your chest.
3. Take 5 slow breaths.
4. Say: "I am safe even when I am still."

Evening: Inner Child Affirmation

Before sleep, whisper:

"You are loved.
You are protected.
You are enough.
You don't have to earn your place anymore."

7-DAY WORTH RESTORATION PLAN

Day 1: Write your earliest memory of feeling "not enough."

Day 2: Identify where that belief came from.

Day 3: Write a new belief to replace it.

Day 4: Practice resting without guilt for 30 minutes.

Day 5: Do something nurturing, not productive.

Day 6: Speak loving words to your younger self.

Day 7: Declare your worth out loud.

LIFE LESSON

You are not valuable because you are strong.
You are strong because you survived.
But your worth was never up for debate.

LIFE LESSON PRAYER

"God,

Heal the places in me that learned to earn love instead of receive it.

Restore the part of my heart that forgot its own value.

Teach me that I am worthy before I work,
loved before I prove,
chosen before I perform.

Let me rest without fear.
Let me receive without suspicion.
Let me live knowing I am enough,
not because of what I do…
but because of who You created me to be.

Amen."

Chapter 6

LEARNING TO BE STILL

When the noise quiets and you finally hear the voice that's been guiding you all along.

For most of his life, Daeron lived in motion.

Moving from house to house.
Moving through environments.
Moving through situations.
Moving through seasons of survival, hustle, ambition, and responsibility.

Stillness wasn't something he trusted.
In stillness, thoughts get loud.
Memories surface.
Questions rise.

So he stayed busy.

Busy keeps you from feeling.
Busy keeps you from remembering.

Busy keeps you from facing the parts of you
that were never given space to speak.

But growth eventually demands silence.

Not the silence of loneliness…
The silence of listening.

There came a season where the noise slowed down.

No streets calling.
No chaos surrounding.
No constant pressure to react.

Just space.

And in that space, Daeron began to notice something he had
ignored for years:

His own inner voice.

Not the voice of fear.
Not the voice of survival.
Not the voice of insecurity.

The voice of wisdom.

The voice that whispered:
"Slow down."
"Pay attention."
"There's more here."
"You don't have to run anymore."

For a man raised in motion, stillness felt uncomfortable at first.
Almost unsafe.

Because when you grow up in environments where danger is real,
your nervous system learns to stay alert.
Rest feels foreign.
Peace feels unfamiliar.
Calm feels suspicious.

But stillness is where healing begins.

It's where you finally hear:

What you truly want.
What you truly fear.
What you truly need.
What God has been trying to tell you beneath the noise.

Daeron learned that the same mind that once had to scan for
danger could now be trained to scan for direction.

Silence stopped being empty.
It became sacred.

HOW TO KNOW THIS CHAPTER IS ABOUT YOU

This chapter is for you if:

- You stay busy to avoid feeling
- Silence makes you uneasy
- You're always in "go mode"
- You find it hard to rest without guilt
- Your mind races when you try to be still
- You sense that clarity is waiting, but you don't slow down enough to receive it

WHAT'S REALLY HAPPENING

Your nervous system learned:

"Stillness equals danger."
"Quiet means something is wrong."
"Rest makes you vulnerable."

But your soul is learning:

"Stillness equals safety."
"Quiet is where clarity lives."
"Rest is where strength is restored."

DAILY PRACTICE – TRAINING THE MIND TO BE STILL

Morning – 5 Minutes of Presence

Before your phone, before the world:

Sit quietly.
Breathe slowly.
Inhale for 4.
Hold for 2.
Exhale for 6.

Say silently:
"I am safe to be still."

Midday – Mental Pause

Set an alarm once a day.

When it goes off:

- Close your eyes.
- Take 3 slow breaths.
- Ask: "What am I feeling right now?"
- Don't fix it. Just notice it.

Awareness calms the nervous system.

Evening – Listening Time

Sit in silence for 10 minutes.

No music.
No phone.
No distraction.

Ask:
"What is my spirit trying to tell me lately?"

Write whatever comes.

7-DAY STILLNESS RESET

Day 1: 5 minutes of quiet breathing.

Day 2: 10 minutes of silent reflection.

Day 3: Write down every thought that keeps racing.

Day 4: Release each one with deep breaths.

Day 5: Take a slow walk with no phone.

Day 6: Sit in nature and observe.

Day 7: Pray in silence and listen instead of speak.

LIFE LESSON

Your power is not only in how fast you move.
It is in how clearly you can hear.

Stillness is not weakness.
It is alignment.

LIFE LESSON PRAYER

"God,
Teach me to be still without fear.
Quiet the noise in my mind and the tension in my body.

Help me trust that in silence, You are speaking.
That in rest, You are restoring.
That in stillness, You are guiding.

I no longer run from quiet.
I lean into it.
I no longer fear rest.
I receive it.

Let me hear what I've been too busy to listen to.
And let that voice lead me into clarity, peace, and purpose.

Amen."

Chapter 7

CHOOSING DISCIPLINE OVER COMFORT

When you realize that the life you want is built by the habits you repeat, not the feelings you follow.

There comes a moment in every person's growth when motivation is no longer enough.

Motivation is powerful, but it is emotional.
It rises when you are inspired… and fades when you are tired.
Discipline is different.
Discipline shows up when you don't feel like it.
Discipline is the bridge between who you
are and who you are becoming.

For Daeron, comfort once looked like escape.
Anything that could quiet the pain.
Anything that could distract the mind.
Anything that could give a sense of control
in a world that once felt unstable.

But comfort never built the future he saw in his heart.

He began to understand something life-changing:

The same discipline that kept me alive in survival can be redirected to build legacy.

Survival discipline says:
"Stay alert. Stay ready. Don't slip."

Growth discipline says:
"Stay consistent. Stay focused. Don't quit."

One keeps you from dying.
The other teaches you how to live.

Discipline meant waking up when it was easier to sleep.
Training when it was easier to rest.
Studying when it was easier to scroll.
Saving when it was easier to spend.
Choosing long-term peace over short-term pleasure.

And every time he chose discipline, something inside him got stronger.

Not his body.
Not his bank account.

His *identity*.

He stopped asking, "How do I feel today?"
And started asking, "Who am I becoming today?"

That shift changed everything.

HOW TO KNOW THIS CHAPTER IS ABOUT YOU

This chapter is for you if:

- You start strong but struggle to stay consistent
- You know what to do, but don't always do it
- You battle procrastination or distraction
- You choose comfort when growth requires discomfort
- You want more for your life but your habits don't yet match your vision

WHAT'S REALLY HAPPENING

Your nervous system learned to chase relief.

Relief from stress.
Relief from pressure.
Relief from emotion.

But growth requires regulation, not relief.

Discipline trains your mind to say:
"I can do hard things."
"I don't need to escape discomfort."
"I can stay present and consistent."

DAILY PRACTICE – BUILDING THE DISCIPLINE MUSCLE

Morning – Commitment Statement

Say:

"Today, I choose who I'm becoming over how I feel.
I choose progress over comfort.
I choose consistency over excuses."

Write the *one* habit that matters most today:

- Training
- Studying
- Prayer
- Business
- Health
- Family
- Rest

And commit to completing it no matter your mood.

Midday – The 5-Minute Rule

When resistance hits:

Tell yourself:
"I will do this for 5 minutes."

Once you start, momentum often follows.
Discipline begins with starting, not finishing.

EVENING – INTEGRITY CHECK

Ask:

- Did I keep my word to myself today?
- Where did I choose comfort over growth?
- Where did I choose growth over comfort?

No shame. Just awareness.

7-DAY DISCIPLINE RESET

Day 1: Identify one habit that would change your life if done daily.

Day 2: Remove one distraction that blocks it.

Day 3: Set a fixed time to practice it.

Day 4: Track completion, not perfection.

Day 5: Do it even when you don't feel like it.

Day 6: Reflect on how it feels to keep your word.

Day 7: Declare: "I am a disciplined person."

LIFE LESSON

Comfort maintains the present.
Discipline creates the future.

You don't become powerful by feeling ready.
You become powerful by showing up anyway.

LIFE LESSON PRAYER

"God,
Strengthen my will when my emotions are weak.
Teach me to honor my future more than my comfort.

Help me become a person who keeps their word,
who shows up when it's hard,
who builds even when it's quiet,
who stays consistent when no one is watching.

Let discipline become my protection,
my structure,
my path to freedom.

I choose growth.
I choose consistency.
I choose the life You placed in my heart.

Amen."

Chapter 8

LEARNING TO TRUST THE PROCESS

When you stop rushing the harvest and learn to honor the season you are in.

There is a pain that comes when you know you're called for more…
but you're not there yet.

You can see the vision.
You can feel the future.
You can sense the growth coming.

But your current reality still looks like preparation, not arrival.

And that gap can be frustrating.

For Daeron, there were seasons where he felt like he was doing everything right—
praying, working, learning, growing—
yet the results didn't match the effort fast enough.

It felt like:

"I'm changing… why isn't my life changing at the same speed?"
"I'm becoming… why am I still waiting?"
"I'm doing the work… why is the breakthrough taking so long?"

But life began to teach him a deeper truth:

Growth is invisible before it is undeniable.

Roots grow in darkness.
Strength forms in pressure.
Wisdom is built in waiting.

And most people quit in the season where nothing looks like it's working—
not realizing that's the very season where everything is being built.

Trusting the process meant understanding:

Every delay is not denial.
Every quiet season is not punishment.
Every slow season is not failure.

Some seasons are simply *development*.

And development is where character is formed, patience is learned, and faith is tested.

HOW TO KNOW THIS CHAPTER IS ABOUT YOU

This chapter is for you if:

- You feel like you're doing the work but not seeing the results yet
- You are impatient with your own progress
- You compare your timeline to others
- You question if you're on the right path
- You feel stuck between who you were and who you're becoming
- You are tired of waiting but don't want to quit

WHAT'S REALLY HAPPENING

Your mind wants speed.
Your spirit needs depth.

Fast growth can look good.
Deep growth lasts.

The process is shaping:

- Your patience
- Your resilience
- Your faith
- Your discipline
- Your emotional maturity

So when the results come, you're able to handle them.

DAILY PRACTICE – BUILDING TRUST IN THE PROCESS

Morning – Surrender Statement

Say:

"I trust where I am, even if I don't understand it yet.
I trust what is being built inside me.
I trust that my time is coming."

Write:

- What am I rushing?
- What might this season be teaching me?

Midday – Comparison Detox

When you catch yourself comparing:

1. Pause.
2. Breathe.
3. Say: "Their timeline is not my timeline. My path is still unfolding."

Then refocus on your own next step.

Evening – Evidence of Growth

Write down:

- One way you handled something better than you would have in the past
- One mindset that has shifted
- One area where you are more disciplined, calm, or aware

Progress is often subtle before it is visible.

7-DAY TRUST RESET

Day 1: Write your long-term vision.

Day 2: Write what you're learning in this season.

Day 3: List what is being strengthened in you.

Day 4: Release the need to control timing.

Day 5: Practice gratitude for small wins.

Day 6: Speak patience over your life.

Day 7: Declare: "I am exactly where I need to be to become who I'm meant to be."

LIFE LESSON

The process is not the punishment.
It is the preparation.

What is taking time is taking root.

LIFE LESSON PRAYER

"God,

Help me trust You when I don't yet see the outcome.

Give me peace in the waiting and strength in the building.

Teach me that delay is not denial,

that quiet does not mean forgotten,

and that growth is happening even when I can't see it.

Let patience mature me.

Let faith steady me.

Let the process prepare me for what is coming.

I trust the timing.

I trust the shaping.

I trust the journey.

Amen."

Chapter 9

BECOMING THE MAN WHO LEADS

When healing turns into responsibility and your life stops being just about you.

There comes a season when you realize your growth is no longer just personal.

It's generational.

For Daeron, this awareness didn't arrive all at once.
It came slowly, like weight settling on the shoulders.

Not the weight of pressure…
The weight of purpose.

He began to see that every choice he made was teaching something, even in silence.
That people were watching, even when they didn't speak.
That children, family, students, and future
generations were learning from how he handled pain,
money, discipline, relationships, and faith.

Leadership, he learned, is not a title.
It's a posture.

It's how you respond when you're tired.
How you speak when you're angry.
How you show up when it's inconvenient.
How you stay consistent when nobody is clapping.

A man doesn't become a leader when he gets followers.
He becomes a leader when he becomes
accountable to his example.

Daeron had once lived for survival.
Then for success.
Now, he was living for impact.

He understood that his healing was not just for him.
It was for his children.
For his students.
For the people who needed to see what was possible.

Leadership meant choosing integrity when shortcuts were
available.
Choosing patience when ego wanted speed.
Choosing humility when pride wanted applause.

And most of all, it meant becoming emotionally safe.

Because true leadership isn't built on fear.
It's built on stability.

A stable mind.

A grounded spirit.

A disciplined life.

A heart that has been healed enough to guide
others without bleeding on them.

HOW TO KNOW THIS CHAPTER IS ABOUT YOU

This chapter is for you if:

- You feel a responsibility to be an example
- You are aware people are watching your life
- You want to lead your family, business, or community well
- You are tired of reacting and want to respond with wisdom
- You desire respect more than attention
- You want to build something that outlives you

WHAT'S REALLY HAPPENING

Leadership begins internally.

Before you lead others, you must:

- Lead your emotions
- Lead your habits

Leadyour time
Lead your thoughts

Unhealed leaders create chaos.
Healed leaders create safety.

DAILY PRACTICE – LEADING YOURSELF FIRST

Morning – Alignment Check

Ask:

- What kind of man/woman am I committed to being today?
- What would leadership look like in my attitude, not just my actions?

Declare:
"I lead with clarity, integrity, and calm."

Midday – Emotional Mastery

When stress or pressure hits:

1. Pause.
2. Breathe.
3. Ask: "What response would a leader choose right now?"
4. Respond, don't react.

Evening – Example Review

Ask:

- What did I model today?
- Would I be proud if my child or student repeated my behavior?
- Where can I grow tomorrow?

7-DAY LEADERSHIP ACTIVATION

Day 1: Define the kind of leader you want to be.

Day 2: Identify one emotional pattern that needs maturing.

Day 3: Practice responding instead of reacting.

Day 4: Do something honorable when no one is watching.

Day 5: Speak encouragement to someone you lead.

Day 6: Take responsibility without excuse.

Day 7: Commit to being the example, not just the voice.

LIFE LESSON

Leadership is not about control.
It is about consistency.

You don't inspire by telling people what to do.
You inspire by becoming what they can follow.

LIFE LESSON PRAYER

"God,
Shape me into a leader who carries wisdom, not ego.
Teach me to lead first in my own life before trying to guide others.

Heal what still reacts in me.
Strengthen what must stand firm in me.
Refine what must be steady in me.

Let my life be a safe place for others to learn, grow, and believe again.
Make me an example of integrity, patience, and love.

I accept the responsibility of influence.
I choose to lead with humility and strength.

Amen."

Chapter 10

WALKING IN PURPOSE

When you realize your life was never just about survival, success, or even healing... it was about assignment.

There comes a moment when everything begins to make sense.

The pain.
The abandonment.
The chaos.
The hustle.
The mentors.
The exposure.
The discipline.
The waiting.
The leadership.

None of it was random.

Purpose is not something you stumble into.
It is something you *grow into*.

For Daeron, purpose revealed itself when he saw the pattern:
Every season that almost broke him also built him.
Every wound became wisdom.
Every lesson became language he could
use to help others find their way.

He understood that his story was never meant to end with him.

He wasn't healed just to be whole.
He was healed to be a bridge.

A bridge from:

- Poverty to possibility
- Trauma to transformation
- Survival to significance
- Confusion to clarity

Purpose is when your pain gains meaning.

When what you lived through becomes what you live *for*.

It is the moment you stop asking,
"Why did this happen to me?"
and start declaring,
"This happened so something could be born through me."

Purpose is alignment between who you are, what you've been through, and who you are called to serve.

And when you walk in it, life feels different.

Not easier.
But clearer.

Not perfect.
But meaningful.

You stop chasing.
You start building.

You stop reacting.
You start responding.

You stop proving.
You start pouring.

HOW TO KNOW YOU ARE STEPPING INTO PURPOSE

You may be entering your purpose season if:

- You feel a strong desire to help others avoid the pain you went through
- Your story keeps coming up in conversations
- People are drawn to your wisdom, not just your success
- You feel called to teach, lead, build, or mentor
- You sense your life has assignment beyond money and status
- You feel peace when you are serving, not just achieving

DAILY PRACTICE – LIVING ON PURPOSE

Morning – Assignment Alignment

Ask:

- Who am I meant to impact today?
- What part of my story can bring hope to someone else?
- How can I lead with intention, not ego?

Say:
"I am walking in purpose today. My life
has meaning and direction."

Midday – Service Awareness

Look for one moment to:

- Encourage
- Guide
- Teach
- Uplift
- Protect
- Lead

Purpose flows through service.

EVENING — PURPOSE REFLECTION

Write:

- Where did I operate from purpose today?
- Where did I still operate from fear or old habits?
- What is God shaping me for next?

7-DAY PURPOSE ACTIVATION

Day 1: Write your life mission in one page.

Day 2: Identify who your story can help.

Day 3: Clarify your gifts and strengths.

Day 4: Commit to developing one of them daily.

Day 5: Serve someone intentionally.

Day 6: Share your story with courage.

Day 7: Declare your assignment out loud.

LIFE LESSON

You did not survive by accident.
You were preserved for purpose.

Your story is a key.
Your healing is a weapon.
Your growth is a gift to others.

LIFE LESSON PRAYER

"God,
Thank You for carrying me through every season.
Thank You for turning wounds into
wisdom and pain into purpose.

Show me clearly who I am called to serve.
Give me courage to walk in my assignment.
Let my life be a light for those still searching for their way.

I accept the call.
I accept the responsibility.
I accept the purpose.

Use me.
Guide me.
Lead me.

Amen."

ENDING – THE LEGACY

This book was never just about healing.

It was about remembering who you are.

You are not your trauma.
You are not your past.
You are not your mistakes.
You are not your environment.

You are the one who made it through.
The one who chose growth.
The one who broke cycles.
The one who learned to see, to feel, to heal, and to lead.

Your life is proof that pain does not have the final word.

Purpose does.

And now, as you close these pages, understand this:

Your story is still being written.
Your healing is still unfolding.
Your legacy is still being built.

Walk forward with courage.
Walk forward with clarity.
Walk forward with faith.

Because the same God who brought you this far…
is not finished with you yet.

ABOUT THE AUTHOR

Daeron Myers

Daeron Myers' life is a testimony of transformation, resilience, and purpose. Raised in instability, shaped by abandonment, exposed to survival at a young age, and surrounded by cycles that statistically should have swallowed him, Daeron became the one who broke the pattern. What once tried to wound him became the very fire that forged him. Through mentorship, discipline, faith, and relentless inner work, he rewrote the narrative of his life and his family line. Today, Daeron is a serial entrepreneur, a sought-after motivational speaker, and a self-made multi-millionaire who has built multiple successful businesses from the ground up. More than financial success, he is driven by assignment — to awaken others to their potential, to teach them how to master their mindset, heal their past, and build generational legacy. His story proves that you are not defined by where you start, what you survived, or what was taken from you — you are defined by what you choose to become.

www.ingramcontent.com/pod-product-compliance
Lightning Source LLC
Chambersburg PA
CBHW052123090426
42741CB00009B/1929